The ABCs of Inclusion

Written by
Beth Leipholtz

Illustrated by
Anastasiya Kanavaliuk

To Cooper, the one I never knew I always wanted.
Keep shining your light on this world, sweet boy.

ISBN 13: 978-1-63489-596-5

Library of Congress Catalog Number has been applied for.
Printed in the United States of America
First Printing: 2022
Third Printing: 2024

28 27 26 25 24   7 6 5 4 3

Illustrations by Anastasiya Kanavaliuk
Cover and interior design by Anastasiya Kanavaliuk

Pronunciation guide and additional resources available at www.bethandcoop.com.

For media inquiries and information about speaking engagements and school visits, visit www.bethandcoop.com.

Wise Ink
PO Box 580195
Minneapolis, MN 55458-0195

We live in a big world, and not every person is the same!

Sometimes when you meet a new friend,
you might notice they are different from you.
Differences can be confusing at first. But when we
take the time to learn about our differences, we
might find some special ways we are also the same.

is for Arthur.

Arthur was born very early and hadn't finished growing in his mommy's tummy. Because of this, his eyes didn't develop all the way.

Arthur can't see anything. He is blind. Being blind doesn't stop him from doing the things he loves. Arthur is learning to navigate the world by feeling and listening to his surroundings!

B

is for Bates.

Bates has obsessive-compulsive disorder (OCD) and anxiety, so he interacts with his surroundings differently than some people. Bates doesn't like changes to his daily routines. He likes parts of his life to be especially organized. Sometimes he worries a lot.
But Bates has an extra-powerful memory and remembers everything!

C

is for Cooper.

Cooper is deaf. This means he can't hear without help from a machine. Sometimes he likes to shut the world off. He uses his hands to communicate with sign language. He can tell whole stories with just his fingers! Being deaf makes some things a little harder for Cooper, but he also gets to learn two whole languages!

D

is for DJ.

DJ has something called osteogenesis imperfecta. This means his bones are very fragile. He had two metal rods put in his legs to help hold his weight so he can walk.

DJ has had sixteen bone fractures in his lifetime. This is a lot! He has to be very careful when running and playing, but he still likes to do both.

E

is for Emma.

Emma was born with cerebral palsy. This means that her brain can't always tell her body what to do, and sometimes her muscles don't work the ways she wants them to.

It can take longer for her to learn to sit, stand, and walk. Sometimes she might need help from a walker or wheelchair. Emma's favorite thing is reading books and she thinks the sound of sneezes is so funny!

F

is for Finn.

Finn has hydrocephalus, which means that too much fluid can build up outside his brain. Some kids with this condition need a shunt to drain the fluid, but Finn doesn't. He just has to go to the doctor and get a special picture taken to make sure his brain is working okay. Finn can do all his favorite things, like play hockey and dance to silly songs!

is for Gabe.

Gabe has something called fragile X syndrome (FXS). It's not something you can see, but it affects Gabe's development. It may take him a little longer to learn how to do some things, like talk or interact, but Gabe is smart! His favorite color is lime green, and he loves to line toys up in color order.

H

is for Haidyn.

Haidyn was born with Sanfillipo syndrome. Over time,
her body will stop remembering how to do things like
walk, talk, and eat. She will need help to do those things.
Even though Haidyn doesn't talk out loud, her beautiful
eyes communicate so much to her family.

I

is for Isla.

Isla was born with Down syndrome. This happened because she was given an extra chromosome. (A chromosome is part of your DNA, which is like the instruction manual for your body.) This means she may look a little different, and she has extra-pretty eyes! Isla used leg braces and a walker to learn to walk. She works extra hard at therapy, and today she can run around with other kids.

J

is for Jacob.

Jacob has a sensory processing disorder. This means that sometimes his senses get overwhelmed. (Senses help us see, hear, smell, taste, and feel!) Jacob doesn't like noises that are too loud or lights that are too bright, but he loves anything that vibrates on his hands, especially vacuums.

K

is for Keaton.

Keaton has something called Mowat-Wilson syndrome.
Keaton hasn't learned to talk yet, but he works with a special
teacher to learn how. Someday he will use a machine called an
AAC to help express himself.
Even though Keaton doesn't talk, he loves being around people!

L

is for Lily.

Lily has Moebius syndrome and uses a wheelchair to move around.
She can't move her face to show her emotions because her nerves
don't work quite right.

Nerves are all over your body, and they help tell your brain what your
body should do. Nerves also help your body feel things. Even though
her muscles don't let her smile, she can still tell you when she is happy!

M

is for My'kiah.

My'kiah has albinism, which means her body doesn't make enough melanin. Melanin is what gives your hair and skin different colors. Albinism also changes how a person can see. My'kiah is blind, so she can't see as much as most kids. She still sees some shadows and light. Someday she may need to use a cane to walk!

Even though she can't see everything, My'kiah loves to run around and spend time outside!

is for Noah.

Noah's kidneys didn't work the right way when he was born. You only need one kidney, so he had one removed; the other was replaced by one from his mom! This is called a transplant. Noah has to take medication every day to make sure his kidney keeps working. He also has to be very careful not to get sick. Sometimes this means wearing a mask when he goes places. By being careful, he keeps his kidney healthy and working.

O

is for Olivia.

Olivia might look different in a few ways. She has something called achondroplasia. This means she won't get as tall as most kids. Her legs and arms will be shorter too. But Olivia can still run and jump and play. With some extra help, she can do the same things as most kids!

P

is for Phoenix.

Phoenix has diabetes, which means he has to be careful about the food he eats. Certain foods can change his blood sugar. That can be dangerous! Phoenix uses a machine to check this and takes a special medicine called insulin. As long as he is careful, he can eat most foods!

Q

is for Quinn.

Quinn was born with muscular dystrophy. She does a few things differently than others. She uses tubes to breathe and to eat. This helps make sure she gets all the nutrients she needs to grow! She also uses a wheelchair to move around.

Quinn may do things differently, but this doesn't slow her down!

R

is for Ryann.

Ryann was born with a heart that didn't work quite right. She had five surgeries before she was three years old!

The surgeries helped her heart learn to build muscle and pump the blood her body needs. Blood carries oxygen throughout the body and to the brain.

Ryann is like most kids, but she has to be careful to not get too out of breath when running and playing. Making sure her oxygen levels are healthy is very important!

S

is for Sage.

Sage was born without one of her hands, but she has a lucky fin! Since she doesn't have fingers, she uses part of her arm to help her roll over and hold toys. Sage might have to learn to do things differently, but she can still do them her own way.

T

is for Tyrian.

Tyrian has Goldenhar syndrome. This syndrome means some of the facial bones near his lips didn't develop all the way. He had surgery to correct this!
Someday, his spine and organs could also be affected. But today, Tyrian likes to run and play with dinosaurs.

U

is for Urban.

Urban is autistic. Autism is different for everyone and isn't something you can see. Urban likes to do things a certain way. He loves to make friends, but he doesn't always know how, because autism affects his nervous system. That's part of the brain! Urban is very smart, and he can memorize a movie after watching it only once!

V

is for Vannah.

Vannah has CHARGE syndrome. This can create different challenges for kids. Vannah may look a little different because the muscles in her face don't all work. She has had many procedures to help her breathe and move better! She used to eat with a feeding tube, but now she's learned how to eat with her mouth.

is for Weston.

Weston was born with spina bifida. When he was growing, his spine didn't develop the same way as most babies' spines. This means learning to walk was much harder. Weston uses a wheelchair when he wants to move fast!

X

is for Xochitl.

Xochitl has KAT6A, a very rare syndrome that only 300 people in the whole world have! It affects her muscles, which means she needs extra help standing and walking. Xochitl might have trouble expressing herself sometimes. But she uses English, Spanish, AND sign language to communicate!

Y

is for Yeshwant.

Yeshwant was born deaf, so he can't hear on his own, but he uses cochlear implants. Cochlear implants are a type of electronic device that use magnets. When the magnets are on his head, he can hear! When they are off, he can't. Yeshwant is learning more about listening and talking every day. He is even learning two languages: English and Tamil!

is for Zoë.

Zoë has epilepsy. Epilepsy causes seizures that make her body shake. A seizure can look scary, but the people around Zoë know how to help her if she has a seizure. Zoë also uses a wheelchair to move around. She loves to watch people and hear funny noises!

We live in a big world, and not every person is the same!

That's what makes us special.
So let's learn about each other and celebrate our differences.
There are a lot of new friends to meet.

Beth Leipholtz

As the hearing mother of a deaf child, Beth Leipholtz has a passion for inclusion. Raising her son in both hearing and Deaf cultures has highlighted the importance of creating accessible and welcoming atmospheres for people from all walks of life. Her books aim to create a more accepting and accessible world for our children.

In addition to spending time with family, Beth enjoys Minnesota summers, photography, iced Americanos, CrossFit, and a good old-fashioned book. Learn more at bethandcoop.com.

Anastasiya Kanavaliuk

Anastasiya Kanavaliuk is a Belarusian illustrator living in Poland. She's a big dreamer who talks to the world through illustration. She loves spending time with her family and friends, watching travel videos, and exploring new places.

Our Family's Story

The journey to this book's existence began in October 2019, when our world was rocked by the information that our son, Cooper, was profoundly deaf. The diagnosis was blindsiding and difficult to work through. As a way of processing, I began writing about and sharing our journey on social media. As we gained a steady following, it became apparent to me that so many people had stories to share—and not only that, they had children to educate. Why not create a book that told those stories, but also served to teach children that differences aren't a scary thing? This book has been a labor of love, and my greatest hope is that it serves as a tool to create a more accepting world for our children. —Beth